YET ANOTHER DAY

YET ANOTHER DAY

A PRAYER FOR EVERY DAY OF THE YEAR

J. H. JOWETT

Foreword

In quietness and confidence shall be your strength.

We need a firmer and quieter assurance while we pray. Even in our supplications it is needful to "rest in the Lord." Perhaps it would be a good thing for many of us in our praying seasons if we were to say less and to listen more. "I will hear what God the Lord will speak." Listening might bring restfulness where speech would only inflame us. It is not an insignificant thing that the marginal rendering of that lovely phrase, "Rest in the Lord," is just this, "Be silent unto the Lord."

Rev. John Henry Jowett, M.A

Table of Contents

JANUARY

1

(New Year's Day). My Father, may I experience the great renewal today! May old duties be new! May my sympathies be new! May my aspirations be new! May I have a new heaven and a new earth!

2

My Father, may the world not mold me today, but may I be so strong as to help to mold the world.

3

My Father, be with me at every turning of the road. When the ways are many, reveal to me the way of life, and help me to choose it.

4

My Father, if I am obliged to flee from the tempter today, may I find in Thee my refuge, if I am obliged to stand, may I find in Thee my strength.

5

My Father, I would yield everything to Thee--my thoughts, that they may be purified, my feelings, that they may be sweetened; my will, that it may be sanctified.

6

Holy Spirit, wilt Thou be my Redeemer today? Show me things that are now concealed! Give me glimpses of unexpected glory! Lead me into the truth! May I find delight in my Lord's commandments! May I be an eager disciple in the school of Christ!

7

My Father, save me this day from the perils of the world, the passion of anger and malice and avarice, and all forms of selfish greed.

8

My Father, may my song of thanksgiving be new every morning! May my sense of Thy mercy be ever fresh, that my praise may flow like a gladdening river!

9

Almighty God, wilt Thou give me the entrance into the Heavenly places? May I walk in the light of Heaven! May I breathe its atmosphere and engage in its services! May I taste of its joys and be a sharer in its peace! May my citizenship be in heaven!

10

My Father, may I have the consciousness of one of thy forgiven children! May I know my sin is forgiven by my more fervent love of the good!

11

My Father, help me to hear the Master's call today, when He calls to me in some unpleasant duty, or when He offers me a welcome task.

12

My Father in Heaven, I would remember those whom in prayer I am inclined to forget. I pray for those whom I dislike. Defend me against my own feelings! Change my inclinations! Give me a heart of pity! Give me the purity of heart which finds Thine image everywhere!

13

My Father, teach me not only Thy will, but how to do it. Teach me the best way of doing the best thing, lest I spoil the end by unworthy means.

14

My Father in Heaven, teach me the value of little things. Show me how to consecrate the trifle. Show me how to make each moment light with Thy presence. May I glorify the day by redeeming every minute! Take my moments.

15

My Lord, Thou hast mercifully brought me to another day. May I begin and end it in service and praise! May I wait for Thee in the way of Thy commandments! May I find in obedience the joy of the Lord!

16

My Father, let my obedience today be a pleasure: let my duties be my delights: let Thy statutes be my songs.

17

My Father, may the Holy Spirit accompany me throughout the hours of this day! May His presence illumine my mind and warm my heart! May He teach me how to think and how to speak! May I not offend in speech or in deed!

18

Gracious Lord, wilt Thou lead me into finer sympathy with all things that are noble and good? Take away all the scales from mine eyes. Help me to see all things even as Thou dost see them. May I have the mind of Christ!

19

My Father, help me to remember I do not sorrow alone, in all my griefs Thou art a partner and Thou knowest just how much I can fruitfully bear.

20

My Father, deliver me from all fear which would drain away my strength. May I only have the fear of Sin, which will make me strong and valiant for the truth!

21

My Father, I thank Thee for the word "morning": the long night shall end: sorrow itself shall be worn out: the tears of the darkness shall glisten as the dew in the morning light.

22

My Savior, wilt Thou make me a child of light? Save me from all murmuring and complaint. May I not be a child of night and depression! May I be full of hope and cheer! May the depressed take courage from my quiet confidence and trust!

23

O Lord my God, I would hunger for Thee as for the bread of life! Create within me a keen appetite for the things of God. If I am reluctant about the matters of the kingdom, intensify my desire. Kindle my zeal. May I awake to righteousness, and sin not!

24

My Father, what message hast Thou for me today? May I be in the Spirit, that I may receive it! Give me the hearing ear. Give me the understanding heart. May I be able to appreciate the truth! May I be at home in the Gospel!

25

My Father, I have heard of the river of water of life. May it pour into my life in refreshing flood today! May it cleanse me of my sin! May it revive the withered flowers! May every virtue be restored! May I be like a well-watered garden!

26

My Savior, may I be one of Thy true disciples! May I not desert Thee on the dark and cloudy day! May I be willing to bear my cross and not seek the way of ease! May Calvary not turn me aside! May I be willing to be crucified!

27

O God, lift me into the light today! May I not walk in darkness! May my mind and heart be illumined by Thy most cheery grace! May thought and speech and deed be lit up that men may see that I am a child of light! Deliver me from the bondage of the night!

28

Holy Spirit, Thou hast gifts for men. Thou hast the gift of peace. Thine is the gift of joy, and Thine the gift of rest. I come to Thee in my poverty, without money and without strength. Graciously grant to me Thy gift! Make me rich for evermore!

29

O Lord, my God, what is Thy will for me today? What task hast Thou for me? What opportunity hast Thou placed in my way? Open mine eyes that I may discover Thy will! Save me from wasting the new day! May I turn it into eternal profit!

30

Heavenly Father, I thank Thee for Thy care. Thy mercies are without number. Thou crownest the day with Thy goodness. Help me to see all the tokens of Thy grace! Deliver me from blindness! May I see the prints of Thy feet everywhere!

31

My Father, teach me the value of little times and of little things! May I know the worth of the moment and the trifle! May I light every deed with the light of life! May every moment go away laden with sanctified supplication and service!

FEBRUARY

1

Jesus, my Saviour, may I rise with Thee today! I would be in the heavenly places with Thee. Lift me into the Light, and may I see things I never dreamed of before.

2

My Father, give me liberty in Thy service. I so frequently feel constrained in the doing of the right. Set my feet in a large place, and help me to do the right with a joyous freedom.

3

My gracious Lord, help me with my temptations. May I convert them into occasions of triumph. May every battle-field have the banner of victory waving over it, and may I be more than conqueror!

4

Father, enlarge my sympathies; give me a roomier heart. May my life be like a great hospitable tree, and many weary wanderers find in me a rest!

5

Father, I would that my daily labour might become a spiritual service. May my labour be so pure and lofty that it shall refine my soul!

6

Great God, create in me the spirit of gentleness. Help me to touch the wounds of the world with the delicate sympathy of a nurse. Save me from all unwise severity, and all harshness of judgment.

7

My Father, in all my afflictions may I find Thy treasure! In my night-times may I see Thy stars! In my prisons may I meet Thine angels!

8

My Lord, help me to make a good beginning and a good ending of this day. Gather together its scattered and broken threads of holy purpose, and may it end in gracious consecration.

9

My Father, guide me in the way of life. Help me to perceive that the broad way leads to bondage, and its apparent ease will bring me into eternal pain. Help me to know the right and to love it.

10

My Father, help me to hear Thy voice to-day, when it speaks to me in humble duties, in common-place obligations, in the ordinary courtesies of daily life.

11

My Father, I would delight in Thee! I would not only follow Thee, but do so joyfully! May Thy statutes become my songs and Thy will my ceaseless delight!

12

My Father, teach me how to do Thy will. Help me not to spoil it by doing it in an unwise way. May my righteousness be lovely! May I allure others to Thee by the beauty of my behaviour!

13

My Father, I bring my sins to Thee. Wipe their influence out of my soul, and their name out of the book of Thy remembrance, for Christ's sake.

14

My Father, may this day bring me new vision, new sense of duty, new perception of opportunity, new consciousness of the privilege of being a child of God.

15

Heavenly Father, give me the grace of sympathy. Keep my affection soft and sensitive. Save me from growing hard. May I be easily touched with the feeling of the injustice done to others!

16

My Lord, lift me today into Thy fellowship. Make me a partner in Thy power, Thy joy, Thy rest, Thy peace.

17

My Lord, pour grace into my lips today, that all my conversation may be gracious, and may tend to enrich and sweeten the society in which I move.

18

My Father, I would pray for the outcasts and the neglected. May my sympathies and the sympathies of others be widened, that the lost and the unremembered may be reclaimed! Help me so to live that they may be brought back home.

19

My Father,may my mistakes be my teachers! May my failures be my warnings! Turn the foolishness of yesterday into the wisdom of today.

20

O God, help me to follow hard after Thee. May I not choose the ways of ease! Help me to take the steep road when that is the way of life.

21

Gracious Lord, may my heart be fixed on Thee! Save me from wandering affections, and from all distractions which would impair the beauty and integrity of my discipleship.

22

My Father, purify my motives at the beginning of this day. If anything is unclean within me, take it away. Lift up mine eyes unto the hills, and may my life be a continual ascent.

23

Help me, O Lord, to rest in Thee today. May I not grow impatient! May I be quiet and trustful, waiting Thy will, until the pillar of cloud move, and I am able to follow!

24

I pray that I may this day live in the consciousness that I am a child of God. Help me to think so highly of my relationship that I shall do nothing mean or unworthy. Keep Thou my feet.

25

Great God, may I not be afraid of what the day may bring! May I hide in Thee, and meet everything calmly and confidently with perfect and joyful trust!

26

Holy Father, endow me with true insight this day, that I may see Thee in the trivial round and commonplace, and find Thy will in all the circumstances of life.

27

Father of all, hear me when I pray for my brethren of every race and clime. May the light of the Cross break upon their eyes and hearts, and may their yoke become easy and their burden light!

28

Great God, teach me how to be gentle. May my successes not make me hard, and may my failures not make me bitter! In all my varied conditions help me to be gentle and full of faith.

29

My Father, I would thank Thee for all the bright things of life. Help me to see them, and to count them, and to remember them, that my life may flow in ceaseless praise.

MARCH

1

My Father, teach me how to be grateful. May I see Thy mercies everywhere, and so be moved to give thanks without ceasing! Save me from the spirit of complaint.

2

Holy God, I would present my body to Thee. May I regard it as the temple of the Holy Ghost! Help me to revere the laws of health as the very thoughts and commands of God.

3

My Father, when I am inclined to grow feverish and hasty help me to abide in the shadow of the Almighty. Keep me cool and calm amid the destruction that wasteth at noontide.

4

Gracious Father, give me the spirit of meekness. Save me from all harshness, intolerance, and pride. May I delight to use my strength in carrying my neighbour's cross!

5

Mighty God, I would begin the work of the day with Thee. May my weakness be wedded to Thy power, and whatsoever Thy will may be, may I have the strength to do it with ease and pure delight!

6

O Lord, keep me sensitive to the grace that is round about me. May the familiar not become the neglected! May I see Thy goodness in my daily bread, and may the comfort of my home take my thoughts to the mercy-seat of God!

7

My Father, may sinful hearts find peace today! May weary hearts find rest! May the sorrowladened enter into the fellowship of Thy strength! And may I too share in the benediction!

8

My Lord, teach me how to walk through the ways of time and yet breathe the air of eternity. May the breezes from the hills of God blow down the vale, and in their inspiration may I find my strength!

9

Great God, I would remember my country before Thee. God save the King! May the dews of Thy grace rest upon his mind and heart and may his reign be full of blessing to all his people!

10

Holy Father, may I watch this day for Thine appearing! May I see Thy coming in my joys and sorrows, in the sunshine and in the cloud, in my recreations and my toils!

11

My Father, save me today from any disposition that would destroy the beauty of Thy family life. Help me to be gracious and sympathetic, bearing the burdens of others, and stooping to their needs.

12

My Father, lift me into the heavenly places, that I may today have communion with Christ. May I see His glory! May His beauty woo me into deeper and more fruitful devotion!

13

Gracious God, mercifully take the rent and sin-stained past into the circle of Thy forgiveness. Wipe out the influence of its sore defeats. Deliver me from its guilt and give me peace.

14

My Father, take away every thought that will today spoil my worship and interfere with the flow of my devotional love. May my mind and heart be open for the expression of praise and the reception of grace!

15

Great God, may I not belittle Thee by little thoughts about Thee! Help me to have large conceptions of Thy love and holiness, that I may be allured into a large and sanctified life.

16

Holy God, I beseech Thee to give me a more sensitive conscience; deliver me from little sins that spoil my fellowship with The Give me freedom from secret faults.

17

I pray for the sweetening of our social life. Bless all who have charge of our civic affairs. May they be men of sanctified spirit, counting it their supreme crown to be well-pleasing to Thee!

18

I thank Thee for little children. I thank Thee for the cheer they bring into the heavy, crowded ways of life; I thank Thee for the sunshine they bring into sad and weary hearts. May they keep my heart young and buoyant!

19

Heavenly Father, grant me grace, that I may hate all sin. There is sin that is still pleasant to me, and I turn to it with delight; change my tastes, that I may loathe it.

20

My gracious God, I praise Thee for Thy faithfulness. Thou hast been about me continually. I mourn my indifference and my neglect. I would renew my vow. Help me to be faithful and sincere.

21

My Father, let the light of Thy countenance shine upon me today. May it burn out of me all that is mean and unworthy, and woo into strength all that is gracious and true!

22

My Lord, the Fountain of light give light to me. Make me a child of light, walking in the light as Thou art in the light.

23

Great God, may this be a week of rich growth in the Divine life! May I live in the heavenly places with Thee! May I never descend to anything base or unclean! May my life be spent in the heights!

24

Gracious Lord, may the mark of discipleship be upon me today! May my fellow-men behold the fruits of my communion with Thee! By my gentleness, my pity, my fairness, my holiness, may they know that I am Thine!

25

Gracious God, remember me in my work. If it be Thy will, give me a prosperous day. May all my work be well done. May I turn nothing out half done. May I glorify Thee by honest work!

26

O God, may all my moments and all my days be lived to Thy glory! May this be the brightest of the days--the one most abounding in spiritual fruit! Let the fruit of the light be in all goodness.

27

My Father, if I am beginning this day with any unclean purpose in my heart, take it entirely away! If I am meditating any injurious design against my fellow, may it be now removed!

28

I would this morning remember any who are often forgotten! I pray for all the vagrants who wander about the country. I pray for the gypsies who have no settled home. May they all find their rest in Thee!

29

My Father I would remember my rulers in Thy presence. Save the King! May the burden of sovereignty be eased by The grace! May the Legislature be illumined by the spirit of counsel and of might! May all our laws be the expression of Thy mind!

My loving Lord, I pray Thee to save me from all unworthy fears. May my service be kept from the ravages of unbelief! Save me from the destruction wrought by fretfulness and care. Help me to rest in Thee.

My God, help me to know the sin that most easily besets me. May I not be taken off my guard! May my eyes be open! May I see the tempter even a long way off! May I be ready armed, strong in Thy grace!

APRIL

1

My Father, take charge of my desires. Incline them into Thy will. May they instinctively bend in homage to Thy choice! May they never rear themselves in haughty antagonism to Thee!

2

Holy God, teach me this day how to worship! May my soul be upon its knees! May I discern Thy presence, and be filled with holy reverence and fear! Teach me to pray!

3

My Father, may the heavens be open today! I would have visions of the things of God. Give me power to apprehend and love them. May they be to me as meat and drink!

4

My Father, light up the small duties of this day's life. May they shine with the beauty of Thy countenance! May I believe that glory may dwell in the commonest task!

5

My God, I thank Thee for the opening day, with all its grace and mercy. Help me to remember its lessons. May I not need to learn them over again! May I carry the treasure of this day into my tomorrow!

6

My Father, may I become more brotherly! Release me from the servitude of self. Give me the freedom of love. Let me find my delights in the largeness of my fellowships. May I find Thee in the service of my brethren!

7

My Lord, teach me how to bear my cross without murmuring. I would not be a sour and grumbling disciple. I would learn the secret of cheerful endurance even when I am carrying a heavy load.

8

My Father, give me a sense of Thy forgiveness. May the sin of yesterday not clog my life today! Wash away my guilt, and help me to hate my sin. May I walk with Thee in white!

9

My loving Lord, I would be more gentle! I touch the sores of the world roughly, and I increase the pain! Make me more sensitive, that I may feel the griefs and failures of others, and touch them with the gentleness of Christ!

10

My Father, may the influence and presence of Thy Holy Spirit abide with me today! May every week be as a long Sabbath of unbroken holiness! May every task be sanctified!

11

Spirit of all good counsel, fill my life with holy purpose. Refine my discernment! May I see the good and love it! In all my difficulties make known to me Thy will! May I be a child of light!

12

Prince of peace, I pray that the strife that prevails among men may come to an end. Destroy our divisions! Put an end to our jealousies. Help us to be patient with our misunderstandings. May we seek the things that make for peace!

13

My loving Lord, help me to meet the unwelcome and the unpalatable in the spirit of quietness and strength. May my disappointments be turned into wealth, and my clouds drop fatness!

14

My God, I bring my life to Thee with all its stains and failures. Have pity upon me! Save me from the sorrow that leads to despair; but give me the sorrow that issues in finer devotion.

15

Mighty God, look upon my weakness. Let the fullness of Thy power flow into the empty channels of my impotent heart. Draw me into communion with Thy strength, and make me more than conqueror.

16

Heavenly Father, give me a vivid sense of my sonship. May I in some measure realize what it means to be a child of God! May I walk with dignity, never stooping to sin! May I walk as a King's son, and may nothing shameful be found about my garments!

17

God of prayer, I would remember the infirm in Thy presence. Bless all our hospitals, where the lame and pain-ridden are brought under loving and beneficent care. May their ailments bind us all into a deeper and more fruitful fellowship!

18

My risen Lord, this is Thy day. May I grow in grace and in knowledge! May I enter more fully into the mystery of Thy life and death! May I rise with Thee into newness of life!

19

My Father, give me the grace of fair-dealing. Enlarge my heart, that so I may have room for my brother. May I not crowd him out of my thoughts! May I surround him with large and gracious sympathy!

20

Heavenly Father, may the atmosphere of the unseen heaven make the atmosphere of my home! Bind our family life into a strong and enduring fellowship. Drive out everything that makes for division and strife.

21

O God, the work of the day is beginning. May it be inspired by lofty purpose and brightened by the sense of Thy gracious companionship!

22

My Father, may I walk as Thy child today! May the sense of my relationship to Thee fill me with a saving self-respect! May my life be as glorious as my relationship! May I walk as the child of God!

23

Pitiful Lord, I pray for the outcasts of the land. Be gracious to all who are regarded as the offscouring of the earth. Multiply the ministries which seek their salvation. Turn their faces to the light, and purify them from their sin.

24

My Father, let in the light today, as my eyes are able to bear it. May some deeper glory break upon my soul, and may I be won into deeper reverence and devotion!

25

Great God, may Thy gentleness make me great! May I have the greatness of humility, of meekness, of gentleness, and of love! May I not covet the world's greatness if it cost me the crown of life!

26

Gracious Spirit, wilt Thou refine my soul to day? I would be more perceptive of the highest things. May I be able to discern Thy faintest breathings! I would hear the still small voice.

27

Holy God, I thank Thee for the purity of the morning May its freshness only reflect the pure brightness of my spirit! May the light of the eternal day fill my soul with glory, and may the cheeriness of my life proclaim the beauty of my God!

28

Merciful God, I pray for all men and women whose lives are attended with many failures. Be merciful to all who have never tasted the sweets of earthly success. Save them from bitterness of heart. May the sense of Thy companionship be an infinite compensation!

29

Holy God, may the glories of Thy spring-time awake my heart into beauty and song! May all the wintriness of my heart be broken! May all the chill and coldness of my heart be banished by the incoming of Thy Spirit, and may I know the joy of the Lord!

30

God of all grace, I pray for all who mold the opinion of our country. Bless all the editors of our newspapers, and all whose ministry is in the public press. Illuminate their minds, and elevate their lives, that all their writings may be for the glory of their God.

MAY

1

My Saviour, this is the day the Lord hath made. May I be in the Spirit on this Thy day! Help me to rise from my dead self into newness of life.

2

My Father, cleanse my heart from all defilement. Wash out every worldly stain. Restore to me my purity. Give me back the white robe. Help me to walk in the beauty of holiness.

3

My Father, wilt Thou teach me the meaning of true service? Save me from seeking my life in selfish seclusion. Let me go out of myself to find myself. May I experience the joy of sacrifice! May I enrich the well-being of my brother!

4

Gracious Lord, reveal to me my secret faults. Deliver me from the sins of which I may be no longer conscious. Make me true in the inward parts. Cleanse me from all uncleanness.

5

My Father, may the glorious light of Thy gospel flood my soul today! May buried seeds of heavenly power awake into life! May budding graces and virtues grow into fuller strength and beauty!

6

My gracious Redeemer, wilt Thou gather up the fragments of my time? Regard my bits of goodness with pity. Forgive my broken vows. Forgive unfinished work. Let goodness and mercy follow me!

7

My risen Lord, I would know the meaning of Thy peace. I am easily daunted and made afraid. Give me Thine own peace, and may I walk with firm and confident step!

8

My God, help me to look up to the hills today. Save me from all downward looking which would lead me into pitiable living. Give me the lofty look that I may have the elevated life!

9

Gracious Lord, may my live this day abound in missionary influence! May the beauty of my behavior allure others to Thy feet! May they feel the winsomeness of the Christian life, and may I woo them into discipleship!

10

Father of all, I think of the scattered and torn sections of the race. May they be bound together into a loving family kinship! Destroy the things that make for divisions. Give peace in our time.

11

Holy Spirit, illumine my mind today. Deliver me from all obscurity in my thinking about right and wrong. May my thought be as clear as the noontide! In Thy light may I see light! May I walk in the light!

12

My Father, I pray for all who have not had a glimpse of Thy face. Mercifully look upon all who are groping in the darkness. May they touch thy hand even before they see Thy face! Bring them speedily to the open vision.

13

My Saviour, may Thy Holy Spirit breathe upon me to day! May the gracious influence brace me, and lift me into spiritual health! May I draw in breath in the fear of the Lord!

14

Holy Father, I would now consecrate this day's toil. May it all bear the marks of Jesus! May there be nothing of selfishness about it! May I not injure my brother while I earn my daily bread!

15

Heavenly Father, help me to see some of the ministry of the darker things of life. May I discover a friend even in the cloud! May my clouds drop fatness! May my disappointments bear rich fruit!

16

Heavenly Father, I pray for the restoration of my lost sense of wonder. I have ceased to wonder at Thy mercies, and the riches of Thy grace. Renew the lost power. May I see the wonderful in the commonplace, and may my daily bread move me into fervent praise!

17

Gracious Lord, give me pity for the infirm. May sorrow and deformity never become a commonplace! May I ever move towards them in sympathetic response! May I have eyes for the blind, and feet for the lame, and healing for all the sons and daughters of pain!

18

My Father in Heaven, may I live in the consciousness of Thy nearness! May I live as if at any moment the veil may be rent, and I may see Thee face to face! May I be assured that Heaven is only a hairbreadth away, and all its powers are with me!

19

Holy Lord, may I dwell in the secret place today! May I be conscious of the Holy of Holies in all that I do! May the Holy Spirit pervade all my affairs! May nothing be common or unclean! May everything be bright with the beauty of holiness!

20

Pitiful God, I pray for all the infirm in the land. Look graciously upon all the sons and daughters of pain. Make me very gentle and sympathetic, that I may help Thee in the gracious ministry. May I be a child of consolation!

21

My Father, look back upon the past in pity. Forgive the broken vows, the unfinished work, the lukewarm desire after truth. May I repent of my sin! Help me to lift my eyes to the hills, and with renewed devotion follow my Lord.

22

My Father, help me to grow in knowledge of Thee through Jesus Christ. May I see new beauties in Him while I go about my common work! May I catch new glimpses of Him in my ordinary tasks!

23

My Lord, forgive what is faulty in the past, and bless what has been true! May all my best vows be renewed! May broken purposes be taken up again! May the end be better than the beginning, and may the evening be filled with light!

24

My Lord, may I be lifted into the heavenly places today! May I feel the power of the eternal! May the transient I kept in subjection, and may I experience the glory of the immortal life!

25

Mighty God, may the sense of my own weakness be swallowed up in the sense of Thy power! May I measure my foes, not by my own impotence, but by the majesty of Thy grace! May I be more than conqueror through Christ!

26

My Father, prepare me for this day's life. May the unexpected not throw me into panic! May nothing disturb my faith! May I rest in the Lord and wait patiently for Him! May all things work for good!

27

Spirit of all good, I pray that all who have influence in my country may have the gift of Thy gracious illumination. Light up the minds of all who are powerful with their pen, and may their words be winged with elevating and sanctifying power!

28

My Father, wilt Thou rid my heart of all bitterness? If I now begin the day in any ill-feeling, wash it all away. If I am harbouring a sour disposition, sweeten it by Thine own constraining love. Melt away all coolness in the fervour of spiritual affection.

29

My Father, I would have the mind of Christ. Take away all my petty and self-centered thoughts, and give me the large and sympathetic thoughts of Christ. Give me a roomy heart in which my brethren may find hospitality.

30

My Saviour, may my fellowship with Thee today be very real! May I enter into the secrets of the Lord! May I discover riches which have hitherto been hidden from me! Give me the purity of heart that can see Thee.

31

My Father, I would remember all who have the control and teaching of little children. Bless all the teachers of our land. Give them a great conception of their calling. May they confirm their teaching by the gracious influence of their lives!

JUNE

1

Father of grace, let the light of Thy countenance fall on me. May I walk in the light! May it kindle holy impulse and chaste desire! May it fill my heart with the love of truth!

2

My risen Lord, may I know Thy resurrection power today? May I be lifted above the ways of the world! May I live the lofty life! And so may my influence be elevating and inspiring!

3

My Father, wilt Thou control my life to day? Watch the gate of the senses. Direct my seeing and hearing. Bring my thoughts into captivity to Thy thought. Incline mine ear to Thee.

4

My Father, may the end be more glorious than the beginning! In the evening-tide let there be light. Let Thy forgiveness remove the clouds. May I renew my broken vows! Amen, and Amen.

5

My Father, I thank Thee for my daily bread. May my manner of eating it turn it into sacramental feast! Feed me with the Bread of Life. Nourish me with holy inspirations. May I grow in grace and holiness!

6

My Father, may my influence today be for good! May I not be a barrier to any inspiring soul! May my fellowship be elevating! May all with whom I have to do feel the better for my communion! May I lead them nearer to God!

7

My Father, may I appreciate the glory of Thy summer-time. May the beauty of the countryside awaken a yearning for the beauty of holiness! May I aspire after the fruits and the flowers of the Spirit!

8

My Father, I pray for the homes of our country. May children find in their parents their finest examples of holy living. Sanctify the fatherhood and motherhood of our land! May our homes be wells of the Water of Life!

9

My Lord, teach me how to bear the cross. May I not choose the easy way and turn my back upon the needful yoke! Save me from sluggishness. Keep me alert and daring. May I lose my life for others!

10

My Lord Christ, Thy light is sweet. Help me to walk in the light that I may abound in the fruits of the light. May I become a child of light! Light of the world, illumine me!

11

Holy Lord, teach me the meaning of real success. May I not become the victim of the world's ambition! May I esteem holiness more than gold! May aim at the eternal, and may I be successful!

12

My Father, renew my attachment to Thee. Save me from indifference. Deliver me from all formality. May the bonds that bind me to Thee be quick and living! May I be constrained to love!

13

My Saviour, may I be conformed to Thy death, that I may know the power of Thy resurrection! May I be lifted out of my dead self, and rise into newness of life! May this day be to me an Easter day!

14

My Father God, teach me how to hate. May I have a hatred of all sin! May I turn from sin not only because it is unlawful, but because I loathe it! May sin never taste sweet! May it be as bitterness in my mouth!

15

My Lord God, I would learn to be faithful in that which is least. I would consecrate the trifle. I would be more and more scrupulous in the doing of Thy will. Lord increase my faith, that I may have increased power.

16

My Father, help me to believe in the nearness of the spiritual world. When the transient seems terribly real, and the unseen world appears unreal, reveal Thyself to me in special power. May I know that Thou art, and may I rest in holy quietude and trust!

17

Gracious Lord, may I learn the meaning of Thy meekness! Teach me that it is the secret of power. May I discover my strength in aiding the weakness of others! May I find my throne by bearing the yoke of my fellows!

18

My Father, may I see my sins in the light of Thy countenance! May I not estimate them by the dimness of the world's ideals! In Thy light shall I see light. Help me set them in the light that I may recoil from them with intense disgust.

19

Father of all, give me a profound fellowship with all men. May I stand aloof from none! May I be separate from sinners and yet be the sinner's friend! May my sympathy be full of healing and restoring power! May I be touched with the needs of all.

20

Lord Christ, in whom all power dwelleth, give me the power to pray. May I be able to detach myself from the world, and fix my thoughts upon the unseen! May the heavenly places become real and immediate to me!

21

Holy God, may I glorify Thee today! May I do my work as though I were engaged in worship! May I be looking for the Son of Man! If He should fine me at my common toil, may I be well-pleasing to Him! May He see my devotion in the ordinary day!

22

My Father, may my influence today be sweet and wholesome! May I inspire some desponding heart, even when I do not know it, by the quiet confidence of my faith! May some fearful heart take courage because I am not afraid! May I cheer by my cheerfulness!

23

Gracious Father, I would pray for all men whose sense of sin is more powerful than their sense of grace. May they gain the consciousness that Christ is greater than the devil, and that in Him they can do all things!

24

Father of all spirits, wilt Thou deepen the spiritual fellowships among men? May the unseen kinships be stronger than material bonds! May there be a union of hearts! In the sense of common

need, and in the joy of a common Redeemer, may they all become
one!

25

Loving Father, I pray for all who are groping after the light. May
they seek in the right place and in the right way! May they sur-
render their wills to the doing of Thy will, that their eyes may be
washed from all defilement! May they have purity of heart that
they may see Thee!

26

My Father, teach me how see the eternal in the transient. May I
see through the shows of things! May the letter disclose to me the
spirit! May the husk yield to me the kernel! In all things may I see
Thee!

27

Holy Spirit, breathe into my life the breath of heaven. May sweet
things be nourished and matured! May hidden beauties spring
into life, and may my whole being become beautiful with Thy
grace!

28

Holy Spirit, quicken my memory. May I remember Thy mercies
and be thankful! May I remember my failures and be humble! May
I remember Thy grace and be hopeful! Lift mine eyes to the hills.

29

Heavenly Father, wilt Thou remember all Thy people today? May they have insight into truth and visions of Thy glory! Have pity on all who are not inclined to acknowledge Thee. Turn their thoughts towards holiness, and set their feet in the way of truth.

30

My Lord, give me Thy rest. I am easily panic-stricken. The crisis alarms me. The unexpected disturbs me. I would be quiet in the storm. I would be at rest in the sudden disappointment. I would trust and not be afraid.

JULY

1

My Father, I thank Thee that I know Thy face in Christ. Help me to love Thine appearing. May I be watchful for all signs of the divine! May I see Thee in unexpected places!

2

My Saviour, wilt Thou teach me the ministry of salvation? Show me how to work with Thee in saving the world from sin. Control my lips. Direct my steps. Make my life a minister of redemption.

3

My Father, may my life be filled with praise! Make me more sensitive to Thy mercies. May the sound of holy joy ring through the rooms of my soul! May there be new song in my mouth every day!

4

Heavenly Father, all things are revealed unto Thee. I pray Thee to regard me in pity and forgive my sins. Help me to hate sins I confess. May my resolution be my defense!

5

Holy Spirit, quicken the secret springs of my life. May I abound in spiritual willingness! May I rise daily into newness of life! Take all reluctance out of my discipleship. May Thy law be my delight!

6

Gracious Father, Thou knowest my sins. Help me I hate them. I bring to Thee the sins I love. Help me to cast them out. May the pure become the alluring! May the good taste sweet!

7

Lord of all grace, I lift my soul unto Thee. Wilt Thou water it and revive it? May I not grow faint in Thy service! May I keel in such communion with the spring that I may be continually refreshed!

8

My Lord Christ, may I follow Thee this day with the whole heart! May I not be afraid of the cross! May I be ready for crucifixion if that be the way of my Lord! May I lose my life to gain it!

9

Holy Spirit, sanctify my common life. Help me while I earn my bread to purify my spirit! May my labour be prayer! May all my ambitions be aspirations! May I hunger and thirst after righteousness!

10

Holy Father, I turn to Thee for rest. I would forget the feverishness of the busy days. I would enter into peace. Deliver me this day from all petty care, and from all disturbing ambitions.

11

Almighty God, wilt Thou shield me this day from all spiritual danger? May none of my circumstances do me harm! May everything bring me good! May even my apparent enemies endue me with spiritual treasure!

12

My Father, may the river of water of life flow plentifully round about Thy people today! May dry sorrow be refreshed! May hard hearts be softened! May barren lives be made fruitful! May the dead be quickened into life!

13

Holy Spirit, wilt Thou give I me a quickened sympathy? I do not feel the pains of others, nor do I enter deeply into their joy. Help me to get out of myself that I may lose myself in others.

14

My Father, wilt Thou control the going out and coming in of all my days? May I begin my days well! May I end them in triumph! From beginning to end let there be light.

15

Holy Spirit, wilt Tho quicken my dying resolves? If any old vow is waxing faint, wilt Thou rekindle it? May my devotion not fall in the bud, but may I carry it forward into maturity!

16

My Father, may I learn how to pray without ceasing! May my devotion not be infrequent! May my religious life be continuous! May I abide in Thee! May I make Thee my eternal home! May I dwell in the shadow of Thy wings!

17

My Lord, wilt Thou elevate and refine my speech? I want my lips to be Thy witnesses. I want my conversation to be sanctified. I pray that my social intercourse may be pervaded by the spirit of grace. Keep Thou my lips.

18

Father of mercies, I thank Thee for my daily bread. May I never take it as though I had a right to it! May I take it as from Thine own hand! May it be to me the minister of grace! May my common meals be as sacramental feasts.

19

God of all, wilt Thou bless all the families of the earth? Remove the things that make for division. Create the common purpose that makes for peace. Destroy the selfishness that engenders strife. Extend the reign of the spirit of love.

20

Gracious Lord I thank Thee for all softening influences in our land. I thank Thee for the presence of little children. I thank Thee for winsome old age. I thank Thee for all gracious men. I thank Thee for strong men who impress by their gentleness.

21

My Father, help me to begin this day with a great expectancy. I too often drift into the day without any purpose. May I go through this day with my eyes open, looking for Christ! May I see Him in everything that is lovely, and may I love His appearing!

22

My Father, create in me the grace of patience. Save me from irritableness. Save me from all sharp and unkindly speech. Deliver me from the selfishness in which unkindness is born. Make me self-forgetful in the service of my brethren.

23

Gracious Father, I would remember all the sons and daughters of pain. May the remembrance make me sympathetic! May Thy consolations abound towards the sufferers! May they feel the healing influence of Thy presence! By their faith may they be able to endure.

24

My Father, may some glimpse of larger truth be given to me today! May I not be contented with yesterday's revelation! May my windows be opened towards the East, that I may catch the dawn of new days and the coming of new light!

25

Great God, teach me to walk before Thee in reverence and godly fear. Save me from flippancy. May no frivolity intrude into my communion with Thee! May my Spirit be ever upon its knees! May I never lose sight of the great white throne!

26

Lord of glory, wilt Thou raise me into greater spiritual refinement? I would discern the eternal more clearly. May I see the heavenly when it is in close contact with the earthly life! May I always see the things that are above!

27

God of pity, teach me how to ease the burden of the world. Show me how to handle it. May I so live today as to make somebody's yoke easier and their burden light! May I share Thy compassions, and so heal the pain of the broken-hearted!

28

My Father in Heaven, make me feel strong in Thy grace today. May I discharge my duty in the spirit of exuberant health! May I feel abundantly equal to all my tasks! May I be more than conqueror through Him who loves me!

29

Father of mercies, let me ever live in the sense of Thy favour. May I keep ever in remembrance that I am a child of grace! May Thy Holy Spirit keep me sensitive to Thy visitations! May I watch for Thy coming!

30

Holy God, teach us how to deal with sin. Give our leaders wisdom that they may know how to contend with great and vested wrongs. May they not be afraid because of the majestic power of vice! May they confront it with holy courage!

31

God of all power, I pray that the world may be energized by Thy Spirit. Purge out of the human race all its vanities and hatreds. May the Spirit of the world be pure and brotherly! May we be one in the common faith in Christ!

AUGUST

1

My Saviour, graciously give me Thine own mind. Deliver me from every thought that is alien to Thine. Illumine my mind. Make me a child of light. Guide me lest I err and mislead others.

2

My Father in heaven, raise my thoughts to the heavenly places in Christ Jesus. May there be am unfailing aspiration in my life! May all the issues of this day's life make for things above!

3

My Lord God, give me the sense of Thy forgiveness. Help me to turn from the sin forgiven. May I hold no further intercourse with it! May I hold it in stern repulsion!

4

My Father, may Thy kingdom come today, and may I help in the coming! May I be kept from everything that will check the progress of the truth! May I so live as to be the minister of Christ!

5

My Father, teach me the spirit of true worship. Save me from all formality. May I not become the victim of mere custom! May my approach to Thee be reverent and fruitful! May my fellowship with Thy people be sanctified and sweet!

6

My Father, may I live in the light of Thy countenance! May I never lose sight of Thee! It is when I cease to see Thee that I fall away in sin. Help me to see Thee that I may love Thee, and may the gracious vision never be eclipsed!

7

My Lord and God, may I pay homage to Thee today! May I have no will of my own except so far as it is Thine! Deliver me from all selfishness and lift me into the light of life.

8

Father of life, give me life more abundantly. Save me from the impotence that comes from partial living. May all that is within me be alive and praise Thy most holy name! May I be alive for evermore!

9

God of all mercies, impart to me the spirit of mercy. Save me from all harshness. Give me a soft and sympathetic spirit. May I do Thy work by gracious living! May I constrain others to Thee by the beauty of a consecrated life!

10

My loving Lord, teach me how to carry my cross. May I never seek to shirk it! May I not fall in love with the easy way; but may I love the way of duty and follow it, even though it mean a cross.

11

My risen Lord, may Thy word be very powerfully preached today! May the attention of men be arrested, and may their hearts be subdued! May it come like a new message and fall upon the spirit like rain!

12

My Saviour teach me Thy way of doing all things. When I speak, may it be with grace. May my courtesies be sanctified! May the reproofs I give be prompted by love! May I have the mind of Christ!

13

My Father, keep me in the spirit of thanksgiving. May the sense of my desert never supplant the consciousness of Thy grace! May there be a new song in my mouth every morning.

14

Holy Spirit, teach me how to be a worthy citizen. May I have exalted aims! May I seek the common weal! May I lose myself in others! May I rejoice with them that do rejoice, and weep with them that weep!

15

May I attain unto refinement of spirit today through the worship of my God! May the communion of saints lift me into saintship! Or if I am denied this means of grace, may I enjoy the invisible communion of the just made perfect!

16

Holy Lord, give me a sense of Thy nearness. May I know no common hour! May every season be sanctified! May everything be as a transparent veil behind which I may see the King of kings!

17

God of all might, look upon my weakness. Link my frailty to Thee. May the devil not take advantage of my impotence! May he find me endowed with all the power of God! Make me invincible by Thy grace!

18

My Saviour, Thou who didst know the ways of common toil bless my work today. May I do it well as unto Thee! Save me from all deceit. May I be frank and open and reliable! May my work be heavenly sacrifice!

19

My Father, I thank Thee for all the mercies of the past. Quicken my memory that I may recall them. May I see the way of grace along which Thou hast in mercy led me! May Thy mercy awake my praise!

20

My Father, I turn to the day's work, I turn to the earning of my daily bread. May I go to it as to prayer! May my labour be an act of worship! May the spirit of my toil rise as acceptable fragrance to Thee!

21

Father of lights, I thank Thee for every one who brings me any illumination. For all who bring me suggestion, counsel, warning; for all who help me by voice or by pen; for all who lead me into a larger life I give Thee the praise and glory.

22

Heavenly Father, may the air of the heavenly places breathe about the ways of time! May men be braced into holiness by the inspiring presence of Thy Spirit! May the atmosphere of the home and the market be more and more conducive to sanctified life!

23

Father of light illumine the minds of my countrymen. Lead us into ever clearer truth. May knowledge grow from more to more! May we bow before the light we have, that we may be worthy of more! May we walk in the light that we may become children of light!

24

Lord of life, illumine my spirit today. Search out the dark places in my heart and make me a child of light. Draw out my secret sins, and teach me to hate them. Transform my desires if I am yearning after that which is evil. Make me pure in heart.

25

God of love, help me in the darker experiences of life. May they become my friends and not my enemies! May my moments of pain enrich my heavenly treasure! May my bereavements enrich my heavenly fellowships! May the light affliction work an exceeding weight of glory!

26

My Father, I would have a stronger appetite for the right. I turn to it reluctantly when I ought to hunger for it. I turn to it as a sick man to his food when I ought to long for it as thirsty men seek their water. Breathe upon me that my appetite may be restored.

27

My Saviour, wilt Thou teach me Thy way? Come near to me, and begin with me at the beginnings. Teach me just how to get on the right lines of the Christian life. Then keep my face steadfastly towards Thee. May I be a good scholar in Thy school, and may I grow in grace!

28

Father of all men, lead me into the secret places of that great name. May the love that is in it lead me into the brotherliness! May I not call Thee Father, and yet not be a brother. Because Thou art our Father, lift me into the spirit of loving kinship.

29

Eternal God, help me to enter into some experience of the power of the endless life. May the glorious hope keep me patient and full of endurance! May I not grow weary or faint in the heavenly way! May I walk as one who is sure to arrive!

30

Father of glory, I pray that Thy Spirit may pervade all the affairs of men. May all governments and rulerships be under Thy most gracious sovereignty! God save the King. May all who hold authority be animated by pure and lofty ambition!

31

Saviour of the world, I pray for all ministries that are seeking the extension of Thy kingdom. For labourers among the poor, among the outcasts, among the high-born, among little children, in this land, and in all lands, I ask Thy Fatherly blessing.

SEPTEMBER

1

My Saviour, help me to pray for all whom I do not like. Help me while I pray to see the beautiful in them. If I am blinded, take the scales from my eyes. May I see the lovable in my enemy!

2

Gracious Saviour, remove all hindrances to true discipleship which lurk in me. May I love to be near Thee! May I be unhappy if I appear to be drifting away! Keep me by Thy side.

3

Holy Spirit, may my consecration grow deeper and richer every day! May Thy grace have an everwidening dominion! May Thy kingdom come within me! Through me may it come to others!

4

My God, help me to renew my vows. If I am oppressed with my failures, may the pain make me wiser! Save me from despair! Light up my hope. Kindle anew my zeal. Help me to lean upon Thee!

5

My gracious Lord, wilt Thou lead me into Thy truth? Deliver me from all prejudices and bigotry, and may I have an open mind and heart for the reception of Thy Truth! May I love the light and seek it!

6

My Father, give me hope of perfectness. May my defects not lead me to despair! May I be confident of awaking at last in Thy likeness! May I be inspired by the wealth of Thy promises! May I not be afraid!

7

Gracious Lord, teach me how to obtain the secret wealth in all things. Direct me to the spiritual treasure in a flower. May I know how to read the glory of the heavens! May I have that meekness which inherits the earth!

8

My Father, help me to remember Thy holiness. May the great vision keep me from irreverence! May I never lose sight of the great white throne! May my soul be continually upon its knees! May I perfect holiness in the fear of the Lord!

9

My loving Lord, I pray for all young Christians. May their sense of power exceed their sense of difficulty! May they not be dismayed by the strength of the tempter! May their religious life ripen in the light of Thy grace!

10

My Father, wilt Thou lead me into a rich conception of sonship? Being the son of a King, may my behaviour be regal and royal! May there be nothing low and mean about my life! May it be large and full of courtesy, revealing its sonship in its grace!

11

My Father may the beauties of Thy creation influence me to a life of holiness! May I be taught by the flowers of the field! May the birds of the air help me into spiritual harmony. May all Thy glories help to clothe me with light!

12

My Father, may I hear the home call whenever Thou dost speak to me! May it always be as a welcome voice! May I love the sound of Thy summons! If be to hard duty, may I rise with willingness! May I take up my cross and follow Thee!

13

Saviour of mankind, I pray for the lost! May some gracious influence arouse the indifferent! May the callous be softened! May the weary turn their eyes to Thee! May the dead be touched with the glory of the resurrection morn!

14

My Father, Thou canst make an old thing yield new treasure. Make this old day yield new surprises of grace. May I be astonished at the fullness of the river of the water of life! May great multitudes share in the heavenly baptism!

15

God of pity, wilt Thou teach me the breadth and depth of Thy sympathies? Save me from all selfishness! May there be room in my life for the affairs of others! May some tired birds of the air find lodgment in my branches!

16

Father of all, may the sense of Thy Fatherhood control my life today! May all selfishness be exiled from my life! May I be a brother to my fellow men! Save me from all deceit. Deliver me from all unfairness. Make me pure and true.

17

My Father, Thy mercies reach even unto the clouds. Even amid the changeable Thy love is constant. When it seems to be absent it is often present in richest abundance. Help me to believe in Thee. Help me to trust.

18

My Saviour, wilt Thou help me to conquer any besetting sin. If I am finding my delight in it, graciously change my tastes. Give me a strong inclination towards the pure and good. May the holy be sweet unto my taste! May I drink of the river of Thy pleasure!

19

My Father, may I lift mine eyes to the hills! May I not be satisfied with the standards of the plains! May I seek my ideals in the mount! May I breathe the mountain air even when I walk the valleys of time!

20

My Father God, may the light of resurrection mornings break upon my soul today! May I see the new light as I have never seen it before! May the life in Christ shine before me with most alluring beauty! May I be wooed nearer to Him!

21

Holy Spirit, let Thy gracious energy move in every institution that is seeking to lift the world into the light of life. May all elevating enterprises move with power! May they thrill with the influence of Christ! May they bear much fruit!

22

Saviour of the world, I would remember all who are seeking to make Thee known. May their experience of Thy grace breathe added power into their speech! May they have visions which will make their ministry a delight! Through them may the world see Thee!

23

My Father, if today I should meet with disappointment, may I be helped to turn it into spiritual victory! May I not only be calm in success, but calm in apparent defeat! In my tribulations may I glorify Thee!

24

My Lord Christ wilt Thou give me a new vision of Thyself today? Give me to see some beauty in Thy character that I may appropriate it in my life! May I put on a little of Thy grace! May I become a little wealthier in Thy jewels, and richer in the forces of the Spirit!

25

My Father, teach me the meaning of sonship. May I not demean it by any unworthy conception! By thinking highly may I rise to the heights! Lift up mine eyes to the hills. And may my life follow my gaze!

26

My Father, at Thy right hand there are pleasures for evermore May I be able to appreciate Thy delights! May I learn even now to enjoy the things of God! Deliver me from all carnal delights, and set my mind upon the things that are above!

27

My risen Lord, help me to live in the heavenly places with Thee. May I bring the heavenly into the earthly! May all my duties be pervaded with the heavenly spirit! May my life be hid in Thine!

28

My Father, I would pray that the commerce of the world may today be sanctified. May the ministry of trade create ties of deeper fellowship! May the necessities of the body lead us into enriched communion of the Spirit!

29

Father of mercies, wilt Thou gather up the fragments of the past month? Gather up my broken vows and help me to renew them. Look upon my failures and graciously forgive them. Breathe upon me in new inspiration.

30

My Father, wilt Thou deliver me from the sins I love? Save me from my own sinful pleasures! Change my delights! May I drink of the river of Thy pleasures! May I enter into the joy of my Lord!

OCTOBER

1

Gracious God, may Thy world speak to me of Thy love! May the glories of Nature lead me into reverence and love! May the wonderful vesture draw me to still one more wonderful Lord!

2

My Saviour, wilt Thou grant unto me Thine own gift of meekness and lowliness? May I be of a quiet spirit! Save me from the restlessness of spirit which so often leads to panic. May I have the grace of repose!

3

Holy Spirit, breathe upon me Thy reviving breath. May my life awake to nobler activities! May no power lie in unhallowed sleep! May all that is within me praise Thy holy name!

4

Lord Jesus, wilt Thou this day enable me to reveal the power of a meek and dutiful spirit? Let Thy light shine within me, that I may be an ambassador for Thee in the radiance of my countenance. May I speak for Thee in the power of a saintly life!

5

Holy Spirit, if any faculty within me be withered, wilt Thou graciously restore it? If anything be growing within me which ought to be dead, wilt Thou graciously destroy it? May I abound in the flowers of the Spirit! May I be a child of beauty!

6

My Father, help me to remember that I am a member of a great family. May I keep in mind the vast necessities of the race! I pray for all peoples. May the barriers that divide us be destroyed! May we come into a living kinship in Jesus Christ our Lord!

7

My risen Lord, may I rise from the dead today! If there be any faculty lying dead within me, wilt Thou graciously restore it to life? If my affections are only partially alive, wilt Thou quicken them by Thy resurrection power! May I be alive unto God!

8

Gracious Father, I would be a child of light. May there be no darkness in any part of my being! May every power be lit up by the light of Thy grace! May Thy glory shine from every faculty! May all that is within me praise Thy holy name!

9

My Father, I pray that my circumstances may not overcome me. If I am successful may my success not become my blight! If I am disappointed, may my failure not make me sour! May all my circumstances be turned to my profit and to the glory of my God!

10

My Father, may I be helped to strengthen the ties of brotherhood among men to day! May my life tend to enrich human fellowships! May my speech be a bond of union! May my behaviour knit society into a closer communion!

11

Holy Father, may I remember that this day I have to do more than make a living: I have to make a life! May I not spoil the one in seeking to gain the other! May the way in which I earn my daily bread also bring sustenance to my soul!

12

My Father in heaven, I pray that all the heavenly forces on earth may be greatly strengthened and enriched. God bless all good men and women! Give purpose and definiteness to their work. May all their endeavours issue in glorified life!

13

My Father, all my springs are in Thee. It is when I forget the fountain that my soul becomes hard and dry. Keep me in remembrance of the springs. May I drink unceasingly of the river of water of life! I pray Thee give me to drink!

14

Holy Father, teach me the hatefulness of sin. Incline my soul towards virtue. Give me elevated tastes. Help me to see the beautiful and to love it. Give me increasingly wonderful visions of Thy glory. May I see myself in Thee!

15

Gracious Lord, I myself would gracious be. Teach me to see the grace of everything that is pure and tender and true. Help me to hold communion with the flowers. May my spirit bow in reverent awe before the wonders of the night-sky! May I move in homage!

16

Spirit of counsel, wilt Thou give me Thine own inspiring presence today? Illumine my thoughts. Drive out the darkness. Make me a temple of light. May all my motives shine with Thy glory! May my very wishes be like white-robed angel bands!

17

My Father in heaven, may all my conduct be hallowed by Thy Spirit! Save me from everything that is vain and mean. May even the trifles in my life be pervaded by the spirit of holiness! May everything aspire! May everything have wings to lift me nearer Thee!

18

My Lord, I bow at Thy feet in that spirit of submission out of which comes truest freedom. Help me to be Thy captive, that I may be a child of liberty. May I find the delights of life in the doing of Thy will! May I be humble that I may be raised!

19

My Father, may I become a more fervent lover of the truth as it is in Jesus! Save me from indifference. Save me from that familiarity which sees no wonder in His life and death. May I walk with reverence, that new visions may ever break upon my eyes!

20

My Saviour, wilt Thou teach me the power of the smallest ministries? May I not despise the things that are least! May I pay heed to all the courtesies of life! Help me to be kindly in speech, and tender and graceful in behaviour.

21

My Father, teach me ever deeper meanings in the purpose of life. Save me from abusing my days. Give me a sense of the unspeakable value of time. May I so live as to place a jewel in every moment! May the entire day shine like fine gold!

22

My Father, I would today think of Thy children who seem to walk in continual defeat. I pray for those to whom disappointment comes after every struggle. Give them the sense of Thy companionship. May they drink of the river of heavenly pleasure!

23

Father of mercies, I thank Thee for the providences of the month. Open my eyes that I may discern them. May I have keen vision for Thy goodness! May the sense of Thy care never die out of my life! May I see Thy handiwork everywhere!

24

My Saviour, wilt Thou give me Thine own love for all my fellows? Save me from selfishness. May my thought include my brother in kindly ministry! May he live in my sympathies! May I have room for him in my prayers!

25

My Father, may this be a day of light to me! May I have visions of Thy glory! May the revelations of Thyself beautify the round of my everyday life! May I see Thee in such wise that I never forget the gracious unveiling! May I see Thy face!

26

My Father, may I have keener eyes for seeing the lovely! I only see it occasionally. I would see it always and everywhere. Give me Thine own sight. Wash mine eyes that I may see. "Lord, that I may receive my sight!"

27

My risen Lord, may I remember that I may even now live with Thee in the heavenly places! May heavenly light be round about me! May heavenly bread be my continual food! May heavenly companionship be my unfailing support!

28

My Saviour, may I walk with Thee in sanctified joy today. May the light never die out of my face! If disappointment should come to me, may my very defeat be glorified! May my fellows see Thy glory whether I am travelling through the noontide or the night!

29

Father of all, wilt Thou teach me how to promote the well-being of all Thy children? If my outlook be selfish, wilt Thou make it brotherly? May my life be like a house with many mansions, with room for the entertainment of my brethren!

30

Spirit of God, wilt Thou come like the south wind into the garden of my life? Breathe about me in quickening breath. May lovely flowers of grace become more abundant in my life! Convert the desert into a garden.

31

My Father, wilt Thou heighten my thought by showing me what men and women may become in Christ Jesus? Save me from small ideals. Set my mind upon things above. May I be humbly intent upon Thy likeness!

NOVEMBER

1

Gracious Spirit, dwell with me. Inspire my thought today. Make my mind incapable of ungodly thinking. May my mind be the mind of Christ! May all manner of beautiful purposes find their home in me!

2

Holy God, wilt Thou graciously hallow my life? Let nothing be unsanctified. Let every day and every place, and everything wear the beauty of holiness. May there be nothing hid from the heart thereof!

3

My Fatber, I pray for tbe rulers of the town in which I live. May they be men of pure heart and clear vision! Preserve our civic life from all uncleanness. Teach us how to convert the city into the new Jerusalem.

4

My Father, I yield this new month to Thy keeping. May I enter into the gracious meaning of trust in Thee. May I today know the gift of

Thy peace! May I rest in the Lord! May my soul grow calm in the contemplation of the love of Christ!

5

My Saviour, I would praise Thee for the knowledge I have of life and immortality. I thank Thee for the lifting of the veil. May I now walk as a child of the eternal! May I live as becometh a child of the Infinite! Make me worthy to be Thy son.

6

Holy Spirit, I thank Thee for all kindly impulses with which our life abounds. I thank Thee for all graciousness. It is Thy gift. Every thought of holiness is Thine alone. Help me to see Thee in all the common kindlinesses and courtesies of life.

7

My Saviour, what is Thy will for me today? What wouldst Thou have me to do? May I know Thy will and know it clearly! May I love the will revealed! Incline my heart as well as my mind. Teach me, and then teach me to love.

8

My Father, I thank Thee for the power to think. May I not abuse the mighty gift! May my very thinking be a sacrifice! May a sympathetic ministry begin in my mind! May my thought be an apostle of the Christ! May all my thoughts wear the white robes!

9

My Father, may Thy Spirit be my companion today! May I not walk a step alone! Save me from that independence which is fruitful in defeat and sin. May I walk with Thee, and if I am prone to wander graciously restore me to the right way.

10

My Father, help me to survey Thy mercies. May I feel that I walk in an atmosphere of grace! May I know that everything that is worth having I obtain from Thee. May I see the seals of Thy love in the common comforts of the day!

11

Gracious Lord, Thou hast promised to men the gift of peace. May I learn the meaning of Thy promise! May I not be contented with ease, or with the comforts of the world! May I lean upon Thy bresst! May I have the peace which passeth understanding!

12

Father of all, I would remember the town in which I live. Bless all who rule and influence our common life. Lead our leaders. May drunkenness and all lust be banished from our midst! May the goodwill of all help the holiness of each!

13

O Lord my God, lift my eyes to the hills. May I begin the day upon the heights! May the influence of exalted comnnunion elevate all the doings in this day's life! May there be nothing low or degrading! May everything be lofty and ennobling!

14

My Father in heaven, may I hear Thy voice to day! Above the clamour of the crowd may I hear the high calling of God in Christ Jesus! May I never lose the sound of the trumpet! May I hear it in my joys and in my sorrovvs, in my labours and in my rest!

15

God of all grace, teach me the way of continual penitence and holy trust. May there be no gaps in my consecration! May my life be all of one piece! May sin make no rent! May my devotion he complete, including even the things that are least!

16

My Father, I woold be led into the secret presence today. May I see new meanings in old words! May new light shine out of the old page! May I feel as never before the beauty of the truth! May I be wooed into a deeper devotion! May I become more like Thee!

17

My Saviour, may I be able to use words with deeper meaning every day! May I have increasing knowledge of the glory of redemption! When I call Thee Saviour, may it be the calling of the redeemed heart! May there be the note of rejoicing in the speech!

18

Holy Spirit, wilt Thou bring to my remembrance the things I ought never to have forgotten? Sanctify my memory. Quicken its hold upon the good. May it retain its treasures! May the lesson of yesterday not have to be learned over again today!

19

My Father, wilt Thou help me to hold fellowship with Thee every hour of this day? May no moment be unsanctified! May every trifle glow in the light of Thy radiant presence! May nothing be dark and unillumined!

20

O Saviour of the world, lift my thought into the breadth of Thy purpose. Save me from all narrowness of outlook. Let my mind be full of hospitality. Help me to remember and to pity the needs of others in less favoured lands. Let all the nations praise Thee.

21

God of all grace, wilt Thou give me some gift of Thy grace? I myself would gracious be. Take away all roughness and harshness of manner. Give me the loving heart and the gentle touch. May I be able to heal the wounds of men by the soft grace of divine consolation!

22

God of power, wilt Thou endow me for the fight today? May I not he defeated in the first battle May the place of trial be the plac of triumph! May I be more thar conqueror through Christ! Help me to win trophies on every field.

23

Saviour, This is Thy day. May I use it for Thy glory! Teach me the meaning of true worship. Show me how to approach Thee. May I

have the spirit of reverence that I may be able to apprehend! May
it be a day of festival for the heart!

24

My gracious Saviour, I thank Thee for the gospel that tells me
Thou art my friend! May I not despise the friendship! May I seek to
be worthy of it! Help me to lift up my eyes to the hills from whence
cometh my help. May I be drawn to Thee!

25

My Father in heaven, teach.me that heaven is very near, as near
to me as my need. May I not conceive the home-land as being far
away, almost beyond the call of my weak voice! May I think that
even my whispers are heard in the beautiful country!

26

Lord of glory, glorify Thyself in me today. May my life shine with
Thy gracious presence! May even the trifles be illumined! May my
very courtesies wear the beauty of heaven! May all my life be lifted
up into completeness!

27

My Lord and Master, wilt Thou teach me the meaning of Thy
cross? May I enter into the secret of Thy sacrifice! May I be willing
to deny myself! If it be Thy will, may I be ready to accompany Thee
to Gethsemane and Calvary.

28

My risen Lord, keep mine eyes upon the heights. May I dwell with Thee in the heavenly places! Save me from grovelling through my days in selfish meanness. May my days be full of aspiration! May my life move towards the eternal and the sublime!

29

My Father God, may I sit at Thy feet today, and listen with attentive ears to every sound of Thy Voice! Open mine ears that I may discern wondrous things out of Thy Word. May I hear Thy high calling in Jesus Christ Thy Son! May I hear the voice of the Highest!

30

Lord Christ my Saviour, help me to glory in Thy Cross. May I make my boast in the merits of my Saviour! May I find my glory in Thy redemption! Save me from exalting my own service. Deliver me from all self-conceit. May I hide myself in Thee!

DECEMBER

1

O Christ my Lord, may I feel the power of Thy resurrection! May I be lifted out of the death of self into the glory of Thy communion! May to me to live be Christ!

2

God of glory, may some of the light of Thy glory shine through me! May my poor life be transfigured by Thine indwelling! May all the issues of my life be children of light! May all my days minister to the honour of my God!

3

O Christ, my King, help me to bow to Thy lordship in all the doings of my life. May my obedience begin in my thought! May every thought be brought into captivity to Thy will! May the soul bend in reverent and ceaseless homage!

4

O God my Father, quicken my hunger for Thee. If I pray reluctantly, intensify my thirst. May my life be filled with eager aspiration!

May I always be longing for the things of God! Give me Thy peace. Give me Thy joy. May I share in Thy strength!

5

My Father in Heaven, I would remember those whom in prayer I am inclined to forget. I pray for those whom I dislike. Defend me against my own feelings. Change my inclinations. Give me a heart of pity. Give me the purity of heart which finds Thine image everywhere.

6

Almighty God, wilt Thou give me entrance into the heavenly places? May I walk in the light of Heaven! May I breathe its atmosphere, and engage in its services! May I taste of its joy, and be a sharer in its peace! May my citizenship be in Heaven!

7

Holy Spirit, wilt Thou be my Revealer today? Show me things that are now concealed. Give me glimpses of unexpected glory. Lead me into the truth. May I find delight in my Lord's Commandments! May I be an eager disciple in the school of Christ!

8

My Father in Heaven, my life is Thine. May I never regard it as my own. May everything bear Thy name, and may I acknowledge the ownership! May for me to live be Christ! May I seek first His rights and His glory! May I crown Him Lord of all!

9

My Father, may Thy heavenly rest possess my soul today. Let it not be a day taken up with earthly ease or pleasure, but a day of heavenly peace May I enter into the secret place! May I have that fellowship which makes me know the rest of the Lord!

10

Spirit of Holiness, may Thy presence pervade my life today! May everything be sanctified! May nothing be common or unclean! May everything shine with the beauty of holiness! May the trifles glow like stars! May I be a child of light!

11

My Saviour, teach me the meaning of Thy redemptive work. Help me to have no mean thoughts about it. Help me to think about it wisely and reverently, that I may increasingly know its power! May I grow in knowledge that I may grow in love!

12

My Lord and God, incline my heart to love Thee. I am conscious of other leadings. I incline too much to the earthly and the transient. Help me to set my heart upon things above. Turn my ambitions into aspirations, and my lusts into prayers.

13

Father of all mercies, fill my heart with Thine own grace. Save me from all hardness and unwise severity. Give me the grace of gentleness. Make me kindly that I may be able to heal the sores I feel. May I put on the heart of compassion!

14

My Father, all fullness is Thine. I bring my emptiness to the fountain. May I be filled with the river of water of life! Fill my gaps out of Thy wonderful resources. May I become complete in Thee! May I at last awake in Thy likeness!

15

Heavenly Father, may the revelation of Thy glory make a heaven on earth today! May we feel round about us the atmosphere that prevails in Thy Kingdom! May the grace of Thy presence make our sunshine! May we have one of the days of the Son of Man!

16

Our Father, teach me to discern the tokens of Thy love and care. Give me a clear eye that I may read the messages contained in Thy gifts. May I know how to interpret my daily bread! May the common life have its evangel! May everything be a revealer of Thee!

17

Holy Spirit,.help me to believe that all needful things may become consecrated ministries. May nothing which is essential for my life be regarded as unclean! May everything wear a white robe! May the spotless linen be found in every room of my life!

18

My Father in Heaven, teach me how to attain unto rest. Save me from the anxiety that consumes my strength and mars my peace. Give me the grace of repose. Help me to lean confidentially on Thee, and to do all my work in the strength of untroubled trust.

19

Saviour of the world, help me to share in Thy travail and Thy sacrifice. Save me when I am tempted to shirk my cross, and evade my duties. Help me when I am prone to turn my back upon the steep hill, and choose the fruitless way of the plain. Help me to follow Thee.

20

My risen Lord, on this day may I be reminded of Thy crucifixion! May I bear about in my body the dying of the Lord Jesus! May Thy sufferings and Thy death add solemnity and seriousness to my life! May I go softly all my days!

21

Lord of all grace, may Thy kindly Spirit work in the secret places of my life! I would be Thine in the inward parts. I would have no secret chamber of my own. I would give Thee every room of my life. Search me and know me, and make me entirely Thine.

22

Lord of all life, wilt Thou quicken me by the ministry of Thy life-giving Spirit? May no part of my being remain in deadly insensitiveness! May I be alive unto God! May all my powers aspire after Thee, as flowers after the sun!

23

My Father in heaven, may the glory of Thy world proclaim to me the possibility of being equally glorious! May I remember that what Thou canst do for flowers Thou canst do for me! May I not see Thy miracles in the world of Nature and deny Thy power in the world of spirit!

24

Father of all, teach me the meaning of that great word. May my life not mock my prayers! May my brotherliness witness to Thy Fatherhood! May my unselfishness proclaim the wonders of Thy love! May my life lift the eyes of my fellows to Thee!

25

Lord of all mercy, help me to see Thy footprints everywhere. In all the love of human kind may I see Thy gift! In all sweet fellowships and beautiful intimacies and all lovely wedlocks may I see the tokens of Thy tender mercy! May Thine earth reveal Thine Heaven!

26

Spirit of Holiness, teach me how to wait upon Thee continually. May I never be off my guard! May I be expecting some gift from the heavenly places every moment! May I watch lest the sacred thing should come and pass unheeded!

27

God of all grace, I would commend to Thee all who have had a disappointing year. Wherever the heart aches in the sense of failure, wilt Thou send the needed balm? If holy vows have been broken, wilt Thou send the grace of repentance and amendment? May we finish the year in the joys of reconciliation!

28

My Father God, may I sit at Thy feet today and listen with attentive ears to every sound of Thy voice! Open mine ears that I may discern wondrous things out of Thy Word. May I hear Thy high calling in Jesus Christ Thy Son! May I hear the voice of the Highest!

29

Lord Christ my Saviour, help me to glory in Thy Cross. May I make my boast in the merits of my Saviour! May I find my glory in Thy redemption! Save me from exalting my own service. Deliver me from all self-conceit. May I hide myself in Thee!

30

O God my Father, quicken my hunger for Thee. If I pray reluctantly, intensify my thirst. May my life be filled with eager,aspiration! May I always be longing for the things of God! Give me Thy peace. Give me Thy joy. May I share in Thy strength!

31

My risen Lord, may I know the power of Thy resurrection! May it lift me up into loftiness of thought and feeling! May it draw me like a mystic gravitation! May I every moment feel the upward calling in Thee! May my spirit be upon the heights!

Made in the USA
Monee, IL
02 June 2026

51469393R00056